Meet the Horses

American Quarter Horses

by Rachel Grack

Bullfrog Books, an imprint of Jump! Library by FlutterBee

Bullfrog Books

Ideas for Parents and Teachers

Bullfrog Books let children practice reading informational text at the earliest reading levels. Repetition, familiar words, and photo labels support early readers.

Before Reading

- Discuss the cover photo. What does it tell them?
- Look at the picture glossary together. Read and discuss the words.

During Reading

- "Walk" through the book with the reader. Discuss new or unfamiliar words. Sound them out together.
- Look at the photos together. Point out the photo labels.

After Reading

- Prompt the child to think more. Ask: Have you ever seen an American quarter horse? What did it look like?

Bullfrog Books are published by Jump!
3500 American Blvd W, Suite 150
Bloomington, MN 55431
www.jumplibrary.com

Jump! is a division of FlutterBee Education Group.

Library of Congress Cataloging-in-Publication Data

Names: Koestler-Grack, Rachel A., 1973- author
Title: American quarter horses / by Rachel Grack.
Description: Bloomington, MN: Jump!, Inc., [2026]
Series: Meet the horses | Includes index.
Audience: Ages 5–8
Identifiers: LCCN 2025011493 (print)
LCCN 2025011494 (ebook)
ISBN 9798896622291 (hardcover)
ISBN 9798896622307 (paperback)
ISBN 9798896622314 (ebook)
Subjects: LCSH: Quarter horse—Juvenile literature
Classification: LCC SF293.Q3 K64 2026 (print)
LCC SF293.Q3 (ebook)
DDC 636.1/33—dc23/eng/20250612
LC record available at https://lccn.loc.gov/2025011493
LC ebook record available at https://lccn.loc.gov/2025011494

Editor: Katie Chanez
Designer: Molly Ballanger
Content Consultant: Becky Robb Hotzler; Wells Creek Wild Mustang Sanctuary; This Old Horse, Inc.

Photo Credits: MV Photo/iStock, cover; catnap72/iStock, 1; Lenkadan/Shutterstock, 3; Dave G. Houser/Alamy, 4, 12–13; Moment of Perception/Shutterstock, 5; PROMA1/Shutterstock, 6–7; lenkadan/Adobe Stock, 8, 23tl, 23tr; Richard Nantais/Adobe Stock, 9, 23bl, 23br; Ted Wood/Cavan Images/SuperStock, 10–11, 23tm; Kobby Dagan/Shutterstock, 14–15; Jackson Photography/Adobe Stock, 16, 17, 23bm; Hakase_420/Shutterstock, 18–19; Canettistock/Dreamstime, 20–21; Jaco Wiid/Shutterstock, 22; Terri Cage/Adobe Stock, 24.

Printed in the United States of America at Corporate Graphics in North Mankato, Minnesota.

Table of Contents

Fast Horses

Horses race.

They are fast!

They are American quarter horses.

They are big.

They are strong.

Cookie has a tan **coat**. His **mane** is black.

Pippy is **sorrel**.
She has a white **muzzle**.

cattle

These horses **herd** cattle.

Champ races on a track.

He wins!

track

barrel

Zeke runs around barrels.

Will he fall?

No way!

Tex takes off.
His rider **ropes** a calf.

He stops.
He pulls.
Nice teamwork!

Stella is friendly.

She gives rides.

She is a good girl.

We make a great team!

A Look at an American Quarter Horse

What are the parts of an American quarter horse? Take a look!

Picture Glossary

coat
The hair on a horse.

herd
To keep animals together and lead them to a place.

mane
The long hair on a horse's head and neck.

muzzle
An animal's nose and mouth.

ropes
Catches an animal with a rope.

sorrel
A red-brown coat color.

Index

To Learn More

Finding more information is as easy as 1, 2, 3.

1. Go to **www.factsurfer.com**
2. Enter "**American quarter horses**" into the search box.
3. Choose your book to see a list of websites.